IDEAS IN PSYCHOANALYSIS

Exhibitionism

Brett Kahr

Series editor: Ivan Ward

ICON BO

TOTEM BOOKS USA

Published in the UK in 2001
by Icon Books Ltd., Grange Road,
Duxford, Cambridge CB2 4QF
E-mail: info@iconbooks.co.uk
www.iconbooks.co.uk

Published in the USA in 2001
by Totem Books
Inquiries to: Icon Books Ltd.,
Grange Road, Duxford
Cambridge CB2 4QF, UK

Sold in the UK, Europe, South Africa
and Asia by Faber and Faber Ltd.,
3 Queen Square, London WC1N 3AU
or their agents

Distributed to the trade in the USA
by National Book Network Inc.,
4720 Boston Way, Lanham,
Maryland 20706

Distributed in the UK, Europe,
South Africa and Asia by
Macmillan Distribution Ltd.,
Houndmills, Basingstoke RG21 6XS

Distributed in Canada by
Penguin Books Canada,
10 Alcorn Avenue, Suite 300,
Toronto, Ontario M4V 3B2

Published in Australia in 2001
by Allen & Unwin Pty. Ltd.,
PO Box 8500, 83 Alexander Street,
Crows Nest, NSW 2065

ISBN 1 84046 275 2

Typesetting by Hands Fotoset

Printed and bound in the UK by
Cox & Wyman Ltd., Reading

Introduction: Punting on a Summer's Day

Almost twenty years ago, during my apprenticeship as a young university student, I went 'punting' one warm June afternoon with a group of friends on the Isis river in Oxford. Owing to the exceptionally lovely weather, literally dozens of punting parties glided by, and the river soon became very crowded with undergraduates celebrating the completion of final exams. As our boat swerved round a certain winding corner of the river, known locally as 'Parson's Pleasure', a flabby, white-haired, middle-aged man jumped out of some shrubbery on the nearby bank, and he began to undress, exposing his genitals to our party of two young women and two young men. The flasher masturbated frantically as our boat sailed by. My fellow students just giggled with bewilderment. Within a matter of seconds, our punt had turned yet another corner and our flasher, mercifully, disappeared from view. My companions, a mathematician and two students of English literature, appealed to me – the budding psychologist – and asked me whatever might possess somebody to engage in such odd behaviour, in broad daylight, with literally dozens of teenagers sailing by. Sadly, my psychology tuition had ill prepared me to pontificate about the origins of genital exhibitionism, and I suppose that I must have muttered something vague about flashers having an 'unhappy childhood'. I had little sense at the time that indecent exposure represents the most common form of sexual offence and that, in just a few short years, I would be working psycho-therapeutically with exhibitionistic patients in the consulting room, who had been referred by probation services and the courts, to help these individuals understand something about the complicated roots of their illegal and troubling behaviours.

The term 'exhibitionism' derives from the Latin word *exhibere*, meaning 'to display'. The clinical exhibitionist will do just that, displaying his or her genitalia to unsuspecting members of the public, in socially inappropriate contexts, as a perverse means of achieving sexual gratification. Colloquially, we often label such individuals as 'flashers'. In legal terminology, we refer to such offenders as 'indecent exposers'. In the psychotherapy clinic, we tend to prefer the term 'exhibitionists'. Whatever moniker we choose, clinical genital exhibitionism constitutes a very widespread concern for the police, for members of the legal profession, for mental health profes-sionals and for the many members of the public who continue to be victimised, often with highly anxiety-provoking consequences, by practitioners of this particular sexual perversion.

Exhibitionism can be conceptualised as a manifestation of mental illness, as a sexual perversion and as a form of criminality. I prefer to refer to such forms of overt penile or vaginal exposure as 'clinical exhibitionism' or 'genital exhibitionism'. But exhibitionism will never be the sole province of the practising exhibitionist. Each and every one of us has developed a multitude of strategies for exposing ourselves in other, arguably less sinister, ways. For example, how might we understand the flamboyant actress who parades her clothed body on stage, or the spurned mistress of the parliamentarian who sells intimate details of her sexual life to the tabloid newspapers, or the never-ending convoy of confessionalists who appear on television chat shows talking about their alcoholic mothers and cross-dressing fathers? One need not unzip one's trousers in order to be considered exhibitionistic; one can reveal aspects of one's character structure or personality style in an exhibitionistic manner as well. A person might boastfully exhibit the content of his or her mind by showing off knowledge, for example, as many academics will do on a daily basis.

So, although we tend to think of exhibitionism as a

clinical state, it can also be used to describe a form of interpersonal relatedness, often quite maladaptive in its consequences. I remember one student, whom I taught many years ago, who did in fact possess an unusually intricate knowledge of a certain area of psychology. But rather than using her hard-earned pool of facts to illuminate group discussions, she made frantic efforts to dominate every classroom conversation, in a truly exhibitionistic style, showing off highly irrelevant pieces of data, and thus irritating all of her student colleagues in the process. Exhibitionism can occur whilst fully clothed.

I have begun to differentiate between 'clinical exhibitionism', the wilful display of one's private body parts in public, and what I have come to call 'psychological exhibitionism' or 'psychic exhibitionism', the revelation of aspects of one's mind or soul, in an exaggerated or inappropriate manner, often to the exclusion of the needs of others. It would be dreadful if each of us kept our talents hidden for fear of being exhibitionistic, but the psychological exhibitionist takes every opportunity, quite narcissistically so, to dominate conversations and social interactions, often with devastating consequences. Therefore, exhibitionism can constitute a crime, a clinical perversion or a maladaptive form of characterological interaction.

In the pages that follow, I will endeavour to provide a portrait of both the psychiatric and psycho-pathological literature on clinical exhibitionism. I will then present a more detailed treatment of the overtly psychoanalytical literature on exhibitionism and indecent exposure – a body of literature that attempts to explore the underlying dynamic structure and unconscious motivational strands behind genital exhibitionism. I shall then conclude with some remarks on 'psychological exhibitionism', and its meanings. Additionally, I will explore pathological defences against exhibitionism, by examining what I have come to regard as *'psychological inhibitionism'*, namely, a maladaptive defence utilised by people so scared of being noticed, and so fearful of their exhibitionistic strivings, that they actually hide their thoughts and capacities, and thus fester with rage about the possibilities and opportunities that they themselves have foreclosed from their lives.

The Psychopathology of Exhibitionism

The History of Exhibitionism

Troubled men and women have engaged in exhi-bitionistic activity throughout the course of human history, as, for example, in the phallic cults of ancient Rome, although documentation about cases from previous millennia remains sparse. One of the first written records of an act of male genital exhibitionism can be located in the early twelfth-century Chinese novel *Chin P'ing Mei: The Adventurous History of Hsi Men and His Six Wives*, *c*. 1111–27. The novel relates the tale of a young man who had displeased a certain lady, whereafter the aggrieved woman's serving maids attacked the man with a variety of long and short cudgels. In a desperate effort to free himself, he removed his trousers, and the sight of his genitalia caused the maids to disperse. In the fourteenth century, in Geoffrey Chaucer's 'The Miller's Tale', one of *The Canterbury Tales*, we learn of the frisky gentleman, Nicholas the Gallant, who went, 'up the wyndowe dide he hastily, / And out of ers he putteth pryvely, / Over the buttok to the haunche bon'.

In terms of surviving documentary evidence, the nineteenth-century sexologist Iwan Bloch unearthed the records of an act of indecent exposure that occurred as long ago as 1550, when a Commission Against Blasphemy in Venice prosecuted an Italian man called Domenego for having exposed his penis to Venetian ladies during Mass in several local churches.

According to the report, Domenego 'harboured such extreme temerity and impudence that he has again and again dared display his pudendal member'.[1] Antonio Bragadin, Francesco Longo and Antonio Trevisan, the three commissioners responsible for eradicating blasphemy from Renaissance Venice, sentenced Domenego to six months of imprisonment, as a punishment for his 'wickedness', followed by ten years of banishment from Venice and her nearby territories. The commissioners stipulated that should Domenego dare to escape, he would have to be captured; and a reward of 400 piccoli would be offered.

More than 100 years later, in 1663, an English aristocrat, the Honourable Sir Charles Sedley (c. 1639–1701), playwright, poet, essayist and translator, became drunk at the Cock Tavern in Covent Garden's Bow Street, in the presence of his comrades Lord Buckhurst (the future Earl of Dorset), Sir Thomas Ogle and one Mr Sackville. The revellers then proceeded to expose themselves from the balcony of the tavern to the passers-by below. Sir Charles, in particular, undressed himself completely, and he 'harangued the populace in such profane language that the public indignation was wakened'.[2] Samuel Pepys, the celebrated London diarist, noted on 1 July 1663 that Sedley began with the 'abusing of

Scripture and as it were preaching a mountebank sermon from the pulpit, saying that there he had to sell such a powder as should make all the women in town run after him'. The records of his indictment (*Le Roy* v. *Sir Charles Sedley*) charged the inebriate gentleman with 'several misdemeanours against the King's Peace, which were to the great scandal of Christianity'.[3] Chief-Justice Foster considered Sedley's status as 'a gentleman of too ancient a family (from the county of Kent)' and, therefore, as the son of a distinguished baronet, they imprisoned him for only one week and fined him 2,000 marks. Sir Charles re-offended some five years later, in 1668, during yet another escapade with his companion Lord Buckhurst. On this occasion, King Charles II had to intercede on Sedley's behalf.

In reviewing these two prominent sixteenth- and seventeenth-century cases of exhibitionism, one cannot help but notice the lack of psychological insight into either the cause or the precipitating factors for these acts of exhibitionism in an Italian church and in an English tavern. Our forefathers regarded indecent exposure as a form of sin or lewdness, rather than as an expression of psychological turmoil, or as an attempt to communicate some internal distress. Nevertheless, the sense of effrontery remains apparent, and there can be little doubt that Domenego's church ladies and Sedley's Covent Garden strollers became offended by these episodes of flashing.

Such early cases helped to prompt new legislation in Great Britain in the first quarter of the nineteenth century. In 1822, during the reign of King George IV, British parliamentarians revised the Vagrancy Act. A category of vagrants known as 'Rogues and Vagabonds' was developed, whose membership included such diverse characters as fortune tellers, beggars, street gamblers, paupers, men who deserted their families, as well as 'All persons openly exposing in any street, road, Public Place or Highway any indecent exhibition', which became a legal enforceable offence, subsequently published in Section 4 of the Vagrancy Act of 1824. Interestingly, this early injunction incorporates three inter-related terms, 'exposing', 'indecent' and 'exhibition', all in the same sentence, perhaps contributing to the subsequent nosological confusion and to our ongoing use of a multitude of terms to describe flashing, ranging from exhibitionism to indecent exposure, and so on.

Members of Parliament in the House of Commons put the new Act to the test on 10 February 1824, when the Home Secretary, Mr Robert Peel, presented the case of a labourer called William Lotcho, convicted of 'violating the decency of the place', by exposing himself 'to an immense extent in the parks, where virtuous females had been shamefully insulted'.[4] Peel argued for a differentiation between wanton or purposeful exposure, and accidental exposure, which ought not be treated as a criminal offence. The Vagrancy Act of 1824 became revised once more by a Select Committee. On 21 May 1824 our predecessors defined the crime of exhibitionism as 'every person wilfully, openly, lewdly and obscenely exposing his person (in any street road or public highway or in view thereof or in every public place of Public Resort) with intent to insult any female', which remains the basis of our current legal prohibition against genital exposure. This revision introduced the important differentiation between accidental exhibitionism and purposeful exhibitionism. In other words, a husband displaying his penis to his wife in the middle of love-making cannot be convicted of indecent exposure; but a highwayman doing so, or indeed, the aged Oxford academic to whom I referred earlier, could indeed be indicted, because of the wish to offend or shock.

By 1925, Section 42 of the Criminal Justice Act stipulated that the offence of indecent exposure need not occur in a public locality. Insulting a female through male genital exhibitionism could occur either outdoors or indoors, in public or in private, as in the landmark case of *Ford* v. *Falcone* of 1971, in which a man exposed his penis to a female rent collector who had called at his flat for monies owing.

The Work of Ernest Charles Lasègue and Richard von Krafft-Ebing

Although the early legal professionals struggled manfully to define and punish cases of exhibitionism, our ancestors in the mental health field had very few recommendations about the nature and treatment of indecent exposure. The first serious psychiatric contribution to the study of exhibitionism can be credited to the influential nineteenth-century Parisian psychiatrist Professeur Ernest Charles Lasègue (1816–83), whose classic article 'Les Exhibitionnistes' appeared in the medical periodical *L'Union Médicale* in 1877.[5] A former teacher at the Lycée Louis-le-Grand in Paris, who counted the poet Charles Baudelaire among his pupils, Lasègue eventually trained in medicine, and worked as a consultant physician to the Prefecture of Police in Paris, where he acquired an enormous amount of clinical forensic experience.[6] In his key essay on the subject, Lasègue defined exhibitionism as the sudden urge to display one's genitalia in a public forum. According to Lasègue, exhibitionists experience frequent urges to expose themselves, accompanied by sexual excitement. The perpetrators will be men, previously of good character, who do nothing to avoid being noticed. Lasègue observed that in most cases, the exhibitionists make no attempt to pursue a further relationship with the victim, and most offenders possess very little insight into the origins of their exposing behaviours. Perhaps most tellingly, Ernest Charles Lasègue recognised that the exhibitionist exists in a mental state somewhere 'between reason and madness', thus capturing the clinical reality that exhibitionists certainly cannot be described as mentally healthy, but nor can they be classified as overtly psychotic, cursed with hallucinations, delusions and other symptoms of gross mental illness.

Effectively, Lasègue's early clinical observations on exhibitionism still apply to contemporary cases. Modern workers would amend Lasègue's findings slightly, noting that although the vast majority of flashers are men, a small number of women do expose their private parts as well. Furthermore, although current psychological investigators would refrain from the more value-laden use of terminology such as 'good character', we now know that most exhibitionists have had very difficult early histories, often riddled with demonstrable psychiatric problems in childhood.

As a matter of historical interest, Ernest Charles Lasègue distinguished himself not only as one of the first physicians to study clinical exhibitionism, but he also became involved in a priority dispute with the British doctor, Sir William Withey Gull, as to who first discovered anorexia nervosa as a clinical entity.[7] Such information assists us in our appreciation of Lasègue as a pioneer classificationist and descriptive psychopathologist.

Nearly a decade after the publication of Lasègue's landmark contribution, Professor Richard von Krafft-Ebing, the eminent, aristocratic Austrian psychiatrist and sexologist, elaborated upon Lasègue's earlier work. In his magnum opus of 1886, the *Psychopathia Sexualis*, Krafft-Ebing described exhibitionism as an offence against morality, and as a violation of Section 516 of the Austrian Statutes. Krafft-Ebing provided us with very detailed descriptions of exhibitionistic behaviour, such as Case 203, a man called 'L'. This 37-year-old used to tap his exposed penis on the outdoor window pane of a certain kitchen so that the servant girls and children in the house could observe him. In spite of his evocative portraits of clinical exhibitionists, Krafft-Ebing possessed very little understanding of the underlying motivations of his patients, and he dismissed their behaviour as 'silly'. He suspected that exhibitionism resulted from idiocy, transitory insanity, clouded or partial consciousness, or from a state of acquired mental weakness. He also noted an association between exhibitionism and other clinical conditions such as alcoholism, paretic dementia, senile dementia, as well as frotteurism and transvestism.

During the twentieth century, an increasingly large number of psychiatrists, psychopathologists and psychoanalysts began to study indecent exposure with much more seriousness. Now, 100 years later, students of psychology actually possess an enormous amount of data about the origins of exhibitionism, not to mention many ideas about the possible treatment modalities for clinical flashers. I shall now review some of the relevant literature concerning the contemporary psychopathological understanding of exhibitionism.

Diagnostic Considerations

First of all, modern mental health clinicians and researchers have struggled to agree upon a name for the condition at hand. As I have already indicated, medical doctors, psychologists and sexologists have referred to the phenomenon of clinical exhibitionism by a variety of different names throughout the centuries, including exhibitionism, flashing, indecent exposure, exposure of person, obscene exposure, public indecency and male genital exposure. Other terms which mental health professionals have used to describe the phenomenon include lewdness or lascivious behaviour.[8] However, the formal diagnostic term used by clinical psychiatrists is 'indecent exposure'. In the psychotherapeutic literature, by contrast, one will more frequently encounter the term 'exhibitionism'. Other investigators have referred to exhibitionism as one of the so-called 'courtship disorders', which include exhibitionism and voyeurism, as well as rape, obscene telephone calls and toucherism, all varieties of anomalous forms of sexual relating which violate the traditional codes of ordinary pairing.[9]

According to the DSM-IV,[10] arguably the most influential codification of mental illnesses throughout the world, 'Exhibitionism' (diagnostic category number 302.4) can be classified as one of the many different varieties of 'Sexual and Gender Identity Disorders'. The DSM-IV divides all sexual and gender

17

identity disorders into three distinct subheadings, namely, the *Sexual Dysfunctions*, the *Paraphilias* (in other words, that category of behaviours previously known as 'sexual deviations') and the *Gender Identity Disorders*. Briefly, the sexual dysfunctions include any ostensible malfunctioning of the genital organs, whether physical or psychological in origin. The sexual dysfunctions might include: hypoactive sexual desire disorder, male erectile disorder (erectile impotence) or premature ejaculation in men, and vaginismus in women. By contrast to the sexual dysfunctions, the paraphilias include any aberration of either the sexual act or of the sexual object. Typical paraphilic sexual deviations of the sexual act (in other words, consensual genital intercourse) might include exhibitionism, as well as frotteurism, sexual masochism, sexual sadism or voyeurism, among other varieties. Typical sexual deviations of the sexual object (in other words, a living human adult partner) might include fetishism, paedophilia or a category of disorders known as 'Paraphilia Not Otherwise Specified', which includes bestiality, necrophilia and zoophilia. The gender identity disorders include transvestism and transsexualism, and other serious attempts to dress as or to become a member of the opposite gender. Thus, from a psychiatric, diagnostic point of view, exhibitionism will usually be classified as a paraphilia, specifically, a sexual deviation of the act.

The current diagnostic criteria for exhibitionism, as outlined in the DSM-IV, require that the patient will have experienced recurrent, intense and sexually arousing behaviours or fantasies of genital exposure to an unsuspecting stranger. The behaviours or fantasies must have endured for a period of at least six months, in order to receive a psychiatric diagnosis. Furthermore, the behaviours or fantasies or urges must cause clinically significant distress or impairment to the individual's social or occupational functioning, or to other areas of life.

The Descriptive Psychopathology of Exhibitionism

Let us now explore some basic facts and clinical observations concerning the practising exhibitionist. First of all, we must remember that indecent exposure or male genital exhibitionism constitutes approximately one third of all sexual offences committed – thus, it becomes the most commonly perpetrated sexual offence, more widespread than abduction, buggery, gross indecency with a child, incest, procuration, rape, among others, for example. In this respect, indecent exposure represents a very large problem indeed. The vast majority of practitioners will be men, but a small number of women do expose themselves as well. Most of the men who exhibit their penises in public places will do so in front of women – mostly young women or pubescent girls – whom they have not met previously. The culprits, mostly aged between 25 years and 35 years, will display their penis in one of two fashions. One sub-group of flashers, known as Type I, will unzip their trousers, revealing a flaccid penis. These exhibitionists often feel some sense of remorse; but the other sub-group of perpetrators, known as Type II, will display an erect penis, often masturbating during exposure in order to maintain the erection. Some of these more severe exhibitionists will experience overt sexual pleasure and little conscious guilt. According to Dr Graham Rooth,[11] a leading psychiatric investigator in the field of exhibitionism, men from this Type II category will be more likely to commit other crimes as well. Some flashers will speak to their victims, and a small number will attempt to make some sort of physical contact. But the vast majority neither talk to nor touch their victims – instead, they display their private parts, generally anticipating a look of shock from the child or adult female victim.[12]

Even though most practising perpetrators will be young men in their twenties or thirties, we do know that approximately half of all exposers have indicated that their overt, conscious interest in genital exhibitionism began before the age of eighteen.[13] But most will not be caught until they have reached their twenties, presumably due to the increased confidence and internal compulsion to practise this particular form of sexual perversion.

Men who expose indecently will do so at all times of day or night, and in all sorts of locations; however, in spite of the internal pressures that compel these individuals to exhibit, their offending behaviour will be determined, at least in part, by external circumstances and vicissitudes. For example, in a survey of exhibitionists from Denver, Colorado, dating from the early 1970s, some 71 per cent of offenders displayed themselves out of doors, while 29 per cent did so indoors. Of the outdoor exposers, almost three-quarters did so in streets – far fewer in alleys, parking lots, parks or school playgrounds. Undoubtedly, the weather will make some contribution, and it will be of no surprise that April and May proved infinitely more popular months for exposure than December or January. Additionally, fewer men revealed themselves on Sundays than mid-week, and the highest incidence occurred between 3.00 and 4.59 p.m. Exhibitionists also need their sleep![14] An Australian report has suggested that the optimal distance between the outdoor exhibitionist and his victim will be approximately 12 ft.[15] Indoor exhibitionists might expose their penis from behind a net curtain to passers-by on the street, or they may do so from the inside of a parked car.[16]

Incidents of indecent exposure occur not only in Anglo-Saxon cities, but throughout the world. In their survey of exhibitionism in the United States and Guatemala, Professor John Rhoads and Dr Enrique Borjes[17] detected roughly comparable rates of exposure between the countries.[18]

Most exhibitionists will not receive custodial sentences. Of the roughly 1,000 men brought to court each year for indecent exposure in England and Wales, approximately 80 per cent seem not to re-offend, and a mere 1 per cent will be dealt with as overt psychiatric cases under the Mental Health Act. Most perpetrators will be fined or placed on probation. Unfortunately, most cases of indecent exposure will never be reported; therefore, we do not have an accurate perception of the exact number of cases or episodes committed each year. But reports by victims suggest that the problem may be much greater than we have previously envisaged. American researchers Daniel Cox and Betsy McMahon[19] ascertained that over 80 per cent of college women did not report their experience of being flashed to the police.

As personalities, the exhibitionists tend to be timid, lacking in social skills and often quite obsessional. Some remain single, while others have married, although those who have generally reveal poor marital adjustment.[20] Unsurprisingly, the typical exhibitionist, as Lasègue reported more than 100 years ago,[21] possesses little or no insight into his offending behaviour.[22]

Abstruse Variations

In its traditional form, clinical exhibitionism involves the unbuttoning or lowering of trousers and pants in a public setting, generally for the purpose of shocking the intended victim. But other variants of exhibitionism do exist. Several workers have written about the rare form of exhibitionism followed by actual ejaculation onto a person or object, known as 'saliromania'. The saliromaniac will expose his genitalia in public, and then masturbate to orgasm, sometimes on a living victim, but sometimes on an inanimate representation of a woman, such as a statue or even a painting. Dr Frank Caprio, an American psychiatrist, and his lawyer colleague Mr Donald Brenner[23] have reported the case of man who unzipped his trousers in a public library, exposed his penis and climaxed over the back of a woman who had leaned over a bookshelf. After this attack of saliromania, the woman became very distressed, and she developed an anxiety neurosis and a subsequent aversion to sexual relations.

Professor Wayne Myers, the American psychoanalyst, has identified another variant, which he has termed 'photoexhibitionism', wherein a man will carry around a photograph of his erect member, and then display the picture to others. In Myers's case report,[24] the photoexhibitionistic patient under discussion used a picture of his penis as a means of enticing other males as part of a homosexual cruising ritual. Myers's patient used to refer to his photograph as 'my American Express card . . . I never leave home without it'.[25] Other variants include 'faecal exhibitionism', a practice whereby a robber will defecate in the home he or she has invaded, thus exhibiting the contents of his or her bowels as a sadistic offering.[26] Professor Christopher Cordess,[27] a British forensic psychiatrist and psychoanalyst, has written about yet another form of exhibitionism involving obscene telephone calls, wherein the male individual exhibits the often destructive contents of his mind to an unsuspecting female caller on the telephone. Cordess has referred to this form of behaviour as 'verbal exhibitionism', historically known as 'telephone scatalogia'.

Whether traditional in format or more unusual in its manifestation, exhibitionism does not always exist on its own as a form of distressing, maladaptive behaviour. It can also be associated with other forms of psychopathology, such as frotteurism – the rubbing of one's genitals against the body of an unsuspecting person – as well as sadistic sexual fantasies. American researchers Abel and Osborn[28] found a strong co-association between exhibitionism and other perversions, such as frotteurism, paedophilia, rape, transvestism and voyeurism. In some 93 per cent of cases, exhibitionists displayed more than one form of paraphilia, suggesting a very complex and tortured internal world requiring manifestation in a poly-symptomatic manner.

Dr Clifford Allen, a prominent British medical psychologist who flourished in the mid-twentieth century, reported a detailed case of a 25-year-old man who exposed his genitalia to ladies on a train. In addition to his acts of clinical exhibitionism, this young man also masturbated to the point of ejaculation in the London Underground, and he engaged in frotteurism as well. Furthermore, he had had a history of incestuous sexual play with his sister, and he had become involved in episodes of mutual masturbation with other boys during his school years. Most worryingly, perhaps, the patient harboured some extremely sadistic fantasies, which consisted of 'using two horses in a plough and removing their insides and of slitting up a negro and taking out his inside'.[29]

The Victims of Exhibitionistic Acts

As we have already noted, exhibitionists will target large numbers of victims (both women and children of both sexes), and recent research has suggested that we have grossly underestimated the incidence of offending behaviour. In a study of 100 British nurses working in a psychiatric hospital, 44 per cent of women had experienced exposure by a male flasher, some more than once; as many as 51 per cent of these episodes of exhibitionistic assault occurred before these women had reached their fifteenth birthday.[30] A comparable survey of American female college students enrolled in an introductory psychology course revealed that some 32 per cent of respondents had experienced an incident of flashing, 37 per cent of these more than once, quite often between the ages of 10 and 16 years. A substantial 57 per cent of the women in the sample knew of other victims of exhibitionism, whereas a full 63 per cent of the women knew of more than one victim.[31] However, over 80 per cent did not report the experience to the relevant authorities. In a sample of 142 exhibitionists, Abel and Rouleau[32] estimated that these men committed some 72,974 separate offences, thus suggesting that the *average* exposer will flash, quite staggeringly, to more than 513 victims in the course of a career of exhibitionism!

Ordinarily, victims will be young adult women, but perpetrators do expose themselves to children as well. In the early investigation by Arieff and Rotman,[33] 80 per cent of the victims were adult women and 20 per cent were children, whereas in the sample studied by Mohr, Turner and Jerry,[34] approximately 59.75 per cent of flashers targeted adults, and the rest exhibited themselves only to children, or to a combination of adults *and* children.

What impact does exhibitionism have upon its victims? According to the American survey, only 14 per cent of the women described their experience as 'severely' distressing or 'very severely' distressing, which may indicate something of the savviness of a sample of psychology students who have a prior attraction to so-called abnormalities of behaviour. Dr Elif Gürisik,[35] a longstanding Consultant Psychiatrist in Psychotherapy at the Portman Clinic in London, has noted a wide variety of responses from victims, ranging from obliviousness, fascination or an anxious giggle, to the more extreme responses of fear, shock, disgust and horror. Gürisik has also commented that some victims will respond to their perpetrator more actively by ridiculing or verbally abusing the exhibitionist. But some women find themselves deeply psychically injured by the experience. Many victims of exhibitionistic activity become extremely distressed and may feel quite assaulted or traumatised. Some women will suffer further as a result of the anxiety endured by undergoing verbal examinations from police and lawyers, and from providing testimony in court.[36]

A Forensic Psychiatric Perspective

The vast majority of exhibitionists do not perpetrate physical harm upon their victims, but we must never be cavalier with regard to the amount of sadism required to assault a total stranger with one's potentially dangerous and intrusive penis. Therefore, we must be vigilant to the possibility that flashing may be

'Exhibitionism was, for him at least, a fruitless and arid kind of being with somebody at a safe remove'. Fortunately, most exhibitionists do not progress to such extremes of murderousness.

Aetiological Speculations

Psychopathologists and psychiatrists have adumbrated many possible theories as to the origin of exhibitionistic behaviour. Many researchers have speculated that the exhibitionist suffers from some form of physiological, anatomical or neurological abnormality that predisposes him to revealing his private parts in public. In 1962, the British medical psychologist Clifford Allen postulated that exhibitionists suffer from an enlargement of the prostate.[40] More recently, researchers Dr Pierre Flor-Henry and Dr Reuben Lang[41] reported that exhibitionists display certain abnormalities when examined electro-encephalographically.[42] Though certain brainwave pattern differences do seem to exist between a group of exhibitionists and a group of non-deviant controls, the aetiological significance of this finding remains obscure.[43]

The forensic psychiatrist Professor Robert Bluglass[44] studied the childhood experiences of men who later became the more dangerous among the cohort of indecent exposers, namely, those who went on to commit contact offences with their victims. In reviewing what psychiatrists call the 'premorbid' history, in other words, the period before the development of overt symptomatology, most subsequent exposers seem to have had overt psychiatric difficulties in childhood, and many had appearances in juvenile court as well. Traditionally, future exhibitionists have had an unstable history of employment, as well as unsatisfactory sexual relationships with adult partners, and many will have had prior convictions for sexual offences.

Before we conclude these very fragmentary comments about aetiology from a psychiatric, non-psychoanalytical perspective, we must note that although exhibitionistic behaviour generally occurs in young men, it can also occur in very much older men. Although mental health workers agree on very little indeed, by and large, whenever a heretofore law-abiding man exposes himself in middle age or in old age, one should always undertake a neurological examination, as late-onset exposure can often be a peculiar manifestation of arteriopathic or neoplastic brain disease.[45] Even eminent psychoanalysts have had moments of genital exhibitionism. In November 1980, the ailing 67-year-old psychoanalyst, Dr Heinz

Kohut, perilously ill from pneumonia, exposed his penis to the nurses at the University of Chicago Billings Hospital. Nurse Eileen O'Shea remembered that every morning the distinguished theoretician of narcissistic personality disorder would prop himself up in bed, 'stark naked, exposing himself'.[46]

Pharmacological and Behavioural Treatments

As we can see, psychiatric workers have amassed a great wealth of epidemiological and observational data about the male genital exhibitionist. But what can be done, if anything, to provide a cure? During the twentieth century, medical doctors and the courts have prescribed a number of different treatments for indecent exposure, ranging from monetary fines, to hard labour or imprisonment. In the United States of America, punishments for indecent exposure have varied wildly from state to state. In the middle of the twentieth century, in the state of Michigan, for example, exhibitionists would be forced to serve a sentence which could range from anywhere between one day in prison to a lifetime prison sentence.[47]

In addition to prison sentences, physicians have recommended any number of surgical procedures, including prostatectomy, the surgical removal of the

33

prostate.[48] The more common attempts at biological treatment include basic pharmacological intervention, such as the administration of antiandrogens or feminising hormones, the use of more traditional psychotropic drugs such as imipramine[49] and antilibidinal drugs such as cyproterone acetate.[50] Other pharmacological agents used by clinicians over the years have included benperidol, clomipramine, fluoxetine and medroxyprogesterone, as well as serotonin reuptake inhibitors, and neuroleptics such as thioridazine.[51] However, a number of these drugs will produce worrying side effects, such as drowsiness, gynaecomastia (enlargement of the breasts in male patients) and Parkinsonism-type symptoms.[52]

In addition to standard pharmacotherapy, the biologically orientated psychiatrists and behaviourally orientated psychologists have attempted any number of other types of treatment programmes. These have included hypnotherapy, social skills training and cognitive-behaviour therapy, as well as the more controversial forms of behaviour therapy, especially self-regulation, covert sensitisation and the extremely worrisome electrical aversion therapy,[53] involving the administration of electric shocks to various parts of the patient's body. Other workers have used valeric acid to induce nausea in exhibitionists.[54] Finally, clinical psychologists and psychiatrists have also experimented with the so-called shaming programmes, which involve enforced nudity.

In 1977, Dr Ivor Jones and his colleague Ms Dorothy Frei of Melbourne, Australia, published an account of a rather unusual treatment programme, reporting on the rehabilitation of fifteen severe, recidivistic exhibitionists.[55] Based on Dr Jones's earlier work with one patient,[56] the investigators attempted to reverse the pattern of genital exposure by requiring each indecent exposer to remove all of his clothing in the presence of an audience of between five and twelve male and female workers, positioned approximately 4–5 ft away from the exhibitionist. After stripping completely in the presence of so many witnesses, the exhibitionist would be asked to discuss his offending behaviour in detail, as well as talk about his impression of the victim or victims. According to Jones and Frei, 'Sweating is usually so profuse that it runs from the axillae to the legs irrespective of the ambient temperature'.[57] After four sessions of this nature, spaced at weekly intervals, the patient would then be videotaped, and then forced to watch himself undress and discuss his crimes, in the hope that this would mobilise his anxiety about the offences.

Encouraged by the positive effects and reduction in

re-offending reported by the Australian team, Ian Wickramasekera[58] of the University of Illinois School of Medicine in Chicago, extended their work, and he has remained at the forefront of developing the 'shaming' techniques, which do report impressive results. But at what cost to human dignity? Wickramasekera raised the shaming stakes with his exhibitionistic patients by forcing them not only to disrobe in front of five female mental health professionals and two male mental health professionals, but also to masturbate on cue. According to Wickramasekera, 'When I say *one*, you will unzip your pants; when I say *two*, you will get a firm grip on your penis (use patient's own word for penis, e.g., cock); when I say *three*, you will start to masturbate (jack-off, etc.)'.[59] Impressively, Wickramasekera followed twenty-three patients who had completed his shaming programme and it seems that, to the best of the investigator's knowledge, only one of the patients had re-offended, the period of follow-up having ranged from 1 year 8 months to 7 years 3 months. We must be quite cautious in our evaluation of these controversial shaming programmes; and in spite of the positive results trumpeted by these behavioural workers, we must remember that we have no evidence that the remission of flashing behaviours stems directly from the so-called treatment. Even Jones and Frei,[60] in their key study, had to admit that the very experience of being arrested and threatened with imprisonment, as well as the effect of being caught on the patient's marriage, will serve as preventatives of future offending behaviour as well.

The Psychoanalysis of Exhibitionism

Sigmund Freud and His Followers

Although the behavioural psychologists and biologically orientated psychiatrists have undertaken a massive amount of illuminating research into the psychopathology of exhibitionism, very few of them have actually satisfactorily understood the internal world of the exhibitionist. Even though traditional psychiatrists can tell us the time of day at which a flasher will most likely expose himself, these colleagues can tell us very little about the patient's deepest, unconscious motivations. As ever, the study of psychoanalysis helps us here to appreciate with greater sensitivity what lies inside the heart of the indecent exposer.

One can easily laugh at the male genital exhibitionist and castigate him as a 'freak' or a 'pervert', or as a menace to society. It may be difficult to empathise with the exhibitionist, and to acquire an understanding of why he engages in a form of illegal behaviour that he finds quite compulsive. Many psychiatric descriptions of the exhibitionist will portray the patient as sociopathic and cruel; while this may be true to a certain extent, such a sketch fails to appreciate the tremendous amount of private suffering that the male genital exhibitionist must endure on a never-ending basis.

The American psychiatrist Dr Frank Caprio and the lawyer Mr Donald Brenner published the following letter from an Indian exhibitionist, desperate for assistance:

I am an unfortunate creature who implores your help. In everyday life, I am a normal man who does his work (that of a bank clerk) in an irreproachable manner. For two or three months all goes well, but then I am suddenly attacked by a kind of anxiety which impels me to spend hours on end, walking about the streets. I know that is far from being a good sign. Once when I felt an attack coming on, I took refuge in a mental hospital, thinking in that way to escape the inevitable. Alas, at nine o'clock in the evening, the impulse was too strong for me. I was quite lucid, but that man who clambered up the railings and jumped down on the outside was not myself. I was impelled by an invisible force which I could not resist. Out of breath, I ran as far as the suburbs. There, in a deserted street, I saw in the distance a young girl approaching. I hid myself, and I know the rest from the police report. As soon as I found myself near her, I opened my trousers, uncovered my genital parts, and began to masturbate. I remember vaguely that her wide-open eyes and her terrified look excited me to such an extent that I immediately had an ejaculation. At once I regained possession of myself, and I tried to run away but fell into the hands of the police.[61]

The poor man continued his narrative:

I beg of you to tell me if I am mad, if I ought to be shut up in a lunatic asylum, since I cannot be responsible for my actions. I beg of you, also, to explain to the judges that I am not vicious, as they say, but an unfortunate creature who is suffering and who has been severely punished by nature.[62]

One can only be touched by the sheer tragedy of this otherwise worthy citizen, compelled by impulses that he patently does not understand, and that drive him towards sadomasochistic enactments, causing harm to his female victim and to himself. The shame and self-loathing experienced by many male genital exhibitionists can become so intense that at least one patient had himself surgically castrated to avoid further episodes of indecent exposure.[63]

Psychoanalytical workers (psychotherapists and psychoanalysts) have perhaps had a greater capacity to regard the exhibitionist not as an evil criminal, but rather as a tormented and anxiety-riven person. In part, this is because, as far back as 1900, Sigmund Freud, the founder of psychoanalysis, helped people to appreciate that each and every human being possesses strong exhibitionistic strivings. Although most of us never expose our private parts in public places, we do nevertheless find ways of exhibiting ourselves, and of being recognised; furthermore, each of us began life as a naked baby, whose rudimentary genitalia would be displayed for all to see.

In his magnum opus, *The Interpretation of Dreams*, Freud[64] wrote at some length about the very widespread occurrence of exhibitionist dreams containing nudity and genital exposure, which, surprisingly, Freud listed as the very first category of what he described as 'Typical Dreams'. With characteristic clarity, Freud noted that: 'We can observe how undressing has an almost intoxicating effect on many children even in their later years, instead of making them feel ashamed. They laugh and jump about and slap themselves, while their mother, or whoever else may be there, reproves them and says: "Ugh! Shocking! You mustn't ever do that!" Children frequently manifest a desire to exhibit. One can scarcely pass through a country village in our part of the world without meeting some child of two or three who lifts up his little shirt in front of one – in one's honour, perhaps.'[65] Thus, for Freud, exhibition forms an important part of ordinary childhood development.

Five years later, in his seminal monograph *Three Essays on the Theory of Sexuality*,[66] Freud elaborated upon his foundational views about exhibitionism, noting that although the tendency to show off parts of one's body will be quite pronounced in very small children, as we proceed through the complex processes of maturation, socialisation and acculturation, we become increasingly subject to the vicissitudes of repression – no doubt because of the increased dangers that an adult penis can bring – and we control our infantile exhibitionistic urges, which Freud regarded as one of the 'component drives'. He noted, however, that in some individuals, those whom one might describe as sexually perverse, the infantile tendency to exhibit will persist, and the individual will develop into a clinical genital exhibitionist. Freud conceptualised this act as a deviation in respect of the sexual aim. In other words, in the more usual scenario one's sexual urges will be aimed at genital intercourse, but in the case of the exhibitionist the aim will be display, rather than copulation. Freud recognised that sexually perverse people, including exhibitionists, will overtly enact their libidinal desires, while the more repressed neurotics will only fantasise about perverse desires, and refrain from gross forms of acting-out. This clinical reality prompted Freud's extremely famous dictum, *'neuroses are, so to say, the negative of perversions'* [*'die Neurose ist sozusagen das Negativ der Perversion'*].[67]

Freud seems to have had little clinical experience of treating exhibitionist patients, but he certainly knew about them. For example, as early as 1895, in his 'Draft H' on 'Paranoia', written to his colleague Dr Wilhelm Fliess, Freud described the case of a young woman who, whilst tidying up the room of a stranger, suddenly found that the man had exposed his penis, and placed it in her hand.[68] This experience of exhibitionistic molestation, involving contact, became one of the triggers that eventually contributed to the woman's subsequent paranoid, persecutory state.

Although Freud had very few further clinical comments to offer about exhibitionism in his subsequent writings, he did remind us of a story of female exhibitionism, generally considered quite rare, reported in the writings of the French Renaissance novelist François Rabelais, whom Freud held in great esteem, in which a woman revealed her vulva to the Devil, who then ran away in flight.[69] He also took the trouble to pen a short footnote to one of the very first psychoanalytical essays on the topic, Dr Wilhelm Stekel's article 'Zur Psychologie des Exhibitionismus',[70] which appeared in the *Zentralblatt für Psychoanalyse*.[71]

Without doubt, Freud's greatest contribution to the study of exhibitionistic behaviour must be his insistence that each one of us began life as an infant exhibitionist, and although most of us manage to contain the urge to display ourselves unduly, the clinical pervert has failed in this task. But by insisting that every grown-up man and woman has both engaged in infantile genital exposure, and has also derived pleasure therefrom, Freud has helped to humanise the condition, and in doing so, I trust, assists us in our campaign to approach the clinical offender with greater compassion and empathy.

In addition to Freud and Stekel, many of the earliest psychoanalysts undertook illuminating clinical research on the problem of exhibitionism. Dr Karl Abraham,[72] the founder of the psychoanalytical movement in Germany, underscored Freud's observation that exhibitionistic impulses, though 'allowed free expression in early childhood, are subjected to a considerable measure of repression and sublimation later on'. Abraham also noted the ubiquity of penile exhibitionism in boys of 3 and 4 years of age, enjoying the act of urinating in front of mother, showing off their competency and being admired.[73] Freud, himself, reminisced quite candidly about his own personal experience of urinating in front of his parents at the age of 7 or 8 years, prompting the scathing remark from his father, 'The boy will come to nothing'.[74]

Abraham's counterpart in Hungary, Dr Sándor Ferenczi, also wrote about exhibitionism in a number of prescient, pioneering contributions to the psychoanalytical literature. Ferenczi realised that the urge to exhibit one's powerful penis, which might be alluring, has become so deeply repressed that it can become transformed into its very opposite, namely, a fear of looking at oneself, as a defence against showing off. Ferenczi published a very short contribution on 'spectrophobia',[75] the fear of looking into mirrors, which he conceptualised, creatively, as a flight from the potential pleasure of exhibitionism. In his subsequent article on nakedness,[76] Ferenczi reported the case of an hysterical woman who dreamed of undressing in front of her son and washing her naked body with a sponge. He theorised that, in such a circumstance, nudity and exhibitionism might serve as a means of instilling fear. Ferenczi also described the case of a little boy who had difficulty sleeping. In order to frighten the child away, his mother would remove all her clothing in the boy's presence. Ferenczi's work has helped us to appreciate that acts of exhibitionistic undressing, whether in dreams or in waking life, can be perpetrated by women as well as men, and can serve the function of inducing terror.

Many other early psychoanalysts penned papers about the problem of exhibitionism, including such celebrated names in the history of psychoanalysis as Edmund Bergler, Felix Boehm, Dorothy Burlingham, Edith Buxbaum, Ludwig Eidelberg, Ernest Jones, Ernst Kris, Lawrence Kubie, May Romm, Isidor Sadger, Leon Saul, Walter Shindler, and Melitta Sperling. Jenö Hárnik,[77] a much neglected figure, wrote one of the earliest papers that dealt with exhibitionism. Based in part on some clinical observations from Hanns Sachs, the early Berlin psychoanalyst, Hárnik reasoned that, in men, exhibitionism serves an important function, namely, a defence against castration anxiety. In view of the actual vulnerability of the genitalia, especially so during the earliest, long-forgotten years of boyhood, adult men will become temporarily reassured by the act of exhibitionism, which reinforces the idea that one still possesses an intact penis. Hárnik also helped to explain why cases of genital exhibitionism occur so infrequently in women. He suggested that because women experience a sense of shame at not having a penis, as Freud had theorised, they do not wish to reveal their genitalia, thus exposing the shameful absence. Additionally, Hárnik reasoned that although most women do not flash their genitals in the way that some perverse men will do, women exhibit the entirety of their bodies, concerned with physique and adornment, so that they remain permanently on display. Dr Sandor Lorand also recognised the importance of exhibitionism as a defence against castration anxiety in his infrequently cited contribution on 'The Psychology of Nudism'.[78] Lorand, a Hungarian-born psychoanalyst who emigrated to New York City, noted that exhibitionism reinforces one's belief in the potency and security of the penis; by unveiling it to unsuspecting bystanders, the perpetrator can elicit a reaction in the victim, emphasising that the penis does still exist and that it might be very powerful indeed.

Also, Lorand argued that exhibitionism protects the male from his fear of the *vagina dentata* (the vagina lined with teeth) of which the patient might fantasise, but that the exhibitionistic act of exposure still allows him some sexual proximity with women nonetheless.

Clinicians have amassed much data from treatment experiences to support the castration anxiety hypothesis as one of the cornerstones in the development of exhibitionism. Dr Ismond Rosen, a psychoanalyst who treated flashers in psychotherapeutic groups at the Portman Clinic in London, described the case of a man called 'Peter', who suffered from 'constant recurring fantasies that his genitals would be bitten off by sharks in the swimming pool, bath water and bed'.[79] Anna Freud reported the plight of a little boy who began to show off his penis to girls in the local neighbourhood, after he had had no fewer than three separate surgical procedures on three of his appendages, namely, a finger, a toe and his penile foreskin.[80] No doubt the boy's exposure served as an attempt at reassurance against fears of having his fingers, toes or penis cut off by the doctors.

Interestingly, some literary evidence for the idea that exhibitionism defends against castration can be found in Laurence Sterne's classic eighteenth-century novel, *The Life and Opinions of Tristram Shandy,*

Gentleman.[81] At one point, the protagonist needs to urinate so badly that he does so through an open window, which then falls on his exposed member. A rumour begins to circulate that Tristram Shandy has become castrated and, in order to counteract this assertion, Tristram's uncle Toby suggests that he ought to exhibit his penis in the marketplace to prove that he still possesses his genitalia.

The little-known Swiss psychoanalyst Dr Hans Christoffel published two studies on psychoanalytical work with exhibitionistic patients, noting that many lead ostensibly heterosexual lives, but that they will often marry older women.[82] Some of these men will suffer from colpophobia (fear of the vagina), hence the predilection for genital *exposure*, rather than genital *insertion*. For Dr Otto Fenichel, the great encyclopaedist of psychoanalytical literature, exhibitionism serves several important functions.[83] In agreement with Freud, Fenichel regarded indecent exposure as an overcathexis of a partial instinct or component drive, which represented a regression to a more infantile form of sexuality. He also confirmed Hárnik's observations about castration anxiety, suggesting that the act of exhibitionism dispels inner doubts about the durability of one's penis. Further, the act of exhibitionism will ensure that others become fearful, which means that the exhibitionist can become the aggressor, rather than the victim, which he fears even more. Finally, Fenichel speculated that exhibitionism serves as a defence against a powerful voyeuristic impulse, an idea to which Freud[84] had already alluded.

The British paediatrician and psychoanalyst Dr Donald Winnicott reinforced Freud's earlier writings about the ubiquity and normality of phallic display in little boys. He actually referred to this period of oedipal development as 'the phase of swank and swagger'.[85] Other important British contributions include those of Dr Mervin Glasser,[86] a one-time Director of the Portman Clinic, who wrote about deficits in the superego structure of exhibitionists, and those of Dr Christopher Lucas,[87] a psychoanalyst who also treated exhibitionists at the Portman Clinic. In Lucas's important essay on exhibitionism, he too supported the castration anxiety hypothesis, and he noted that exhibitionism also provides relief for the patient from his own internal turmoil. Through evoking fear in the female victim, the exhibitionist succeeds in projecting his own distress into someone else. Lucas described the act of exposure as 'both successful and unsuccessful',[88] in that the revelation of the penis provides relief and sexual stimulation, but it also causes harm to the victim, and ultimately to the exhibitionist and to his family as well.

Modern Theories of Developmental Failure

Throughout the last three decades and more, Professor Charles Socarides, the American psychoanalyst, has developed the most rich and developmentally thorough theory of exhibitionism, based upon his extensive clinical experience with sexually perverse patients. Socarides has theorised that the exhibitionistic perversion functions in large measure as a means of achieving a deeper sense of masculinity in a male who struggles with his own sense of sexual identity.[89] Contrary to many psychiatrists who underscore that most exhibitionists function in heterosexual relationships, Socarides has become aware of the prevalence of homosexual wishes and tendencies in his exhibitionistic patients. Professor Socarides has suggested that, as little boys, the exhibitionists failed to navigate the separation–individuation phase of development, the time when the boy becomes separate from his mother with whom he has enjoyed great closeness. By not having succeeded in traversing the separation–individuation phase, the pre-exhibitionistic boy will become more greatly identified with mother than with father, thus carrying through life a sense of deep masculine inadequacy. The exhibitionistic act will then function as a means of deriving acknowledgement of masculinity, and as a way of reducing what Socarides has described as the exhibitionist's primary feminine identification.[90]

According to Socarides, the exhibitionist has had to endure a very difficult relationship with mother, who, in all likelihood, will have deprived her son of much early infantile care. From the life histories of his patients, Socarides has heard tales of tremendous neglect and abandonment, often resulting in depression in later life. For Socarides, the act of indecent exposure not only serves to ward off feminine impulses and to search for an injection of masculinity, but it also functions to stave off depressive affects as well, especially the exhibitionist's sense of hopelessness.

In terms of early childhood experiences, it seems that exhibitionists might not only experience deprivation of care in the mother–baby relationship, but as the early years unfold, pre-exhibitionist children often become subjected to actual scenes of bodily exposure in the household. Dr Sandor Lorand[91] discussed the case of a 16-year-old girl who would undress completely at petting parties. On one occasion, she encouraged a 20-year-old boy to undress completely, eventually causing him to climax. The girl's mother consulted with Dr Lorand about her daughter's behaviour and it soon emerged that during the 16-year-old's early childhood, this same mother used to walk around naked, as did the children. Therefore, we can surmise that early experiences of nudity and exposure will contribute to a subsequent sense of familiarity with later acts of public undressing. Similarly, Dr Frank Caprio[92] described the early years of a male exhibitionist whose mother used to walk into the bathroom nude, ostensibly in order to comb her hair, whilst her son stood in the shower![93] Caprio's patient, a 19-year-old who had begun exposing his penis as early as 14 years of age, reminisced: 'Sometimes when I was in a bathtub taking a bath, my mother would come in to get a towel. Once or twice when I was taking a shower she would come in to urinate. I could hear her urinating. My father would do the same thing. I could see my mother wipe herself with toilet paper. When I would be shaving, my mother would come in to urinate or defecate.'[94] One discovers these sorts of early experiences with widespread frequency in the families of many exhibitionists. Dr Robert Stoller, the American psychoanalyst who has written so extensively about perversions, published the case of a woman called

'Olympia', a centrefold in the pornographic magazine *Raunch*, who, as a child, used to frequent male toilets with her father, watching the grown men urinating. Olympia's mother also paraded nude around the house.[95]

Christopher Lucas observed, quite tellingly, that several exhibitionists with whom he worked clinically would also be stutterers or stammerers, which prompted him to speculate that these men grew up in homes with limited verbal communication and, thus, developed a tendency to use *action*, rather than *verbalisation*, as means of expressing internal conflicts.[96] I have certainly worked with several mentally handicapped patients who had exhibited their genitalia publicly, and in every case the patients struggled to produce words – acts of exposure came more easily.[97]

Psychoanalytical workers have also made a number of astute observations about the immediate triggers of an exhibitionist episode, usually linking the act to a recent trauma, abandonment or humiliation.[98] Clifford Allen related the case of a man who exposed his penis after a woman rebuffed his marriage proposal.[99] Christopher Lucas wrote about a man who displayed his genitals immediately after having rowed with his wife.[100] And Wayne Myers noted that his photoexhibitionistic patient showed a picture of his erect penis to one of Myers's other patients in the waiting room, shortly after Myers had announced his own forthcoming holiday break.[101]

Summarising the psychoanalytical contributions to the study of exhibitionism as a form of sexual perversion, we can enumerate the following observations:

1. Exhibitionism serves as a communication of internal distress, usually linked to early childhood traumata.
2. Exhibitionism functions as a defence against castration anxiety, and as a means of reinforcing masculine potency.
3. Exhibitionism protects the patient from intercourse with women who may be conceived as dangerous or castrating.
4. Exhibitionism protects the patient against homosexuality.
5. Exhibitionism permits the patient to express sadism towards women, especially hatred toward the mother.
6. Exhibitionism functions as narcissistic display.
7. Exhibitionism expresses the patient's masochistic tendencies, and his need to court capture by police and other authorities, thus gratifying the desire to be punished.

8. Exhibitionism serves as a means of restoring the patient's damaged self-esteem.
9. Exhibitionism permits the patient to transform aggressive affects into sexual affects.

Clinical Exhibitionism in Women

Before we conclude our survey of psychoanalytical research on exhibitionism, let us examine in somewhat greater detail the problem of female exhibitionism. For many years, psychoanalysts did not believe that women ever exhibited themselves. Even Dr Ismond Rosen, an immensely erudite student of the world literature on the subject, stated, quite categorically, that, 'The perversion of genital exhibitionism does not occur in women.'[102] However, as early as 1945, Otto Fenichel did discuss the story of a woman who cut a piece of fabric out of her dress, both to exhibit her genitals and to facilitate cunnilingus.[103] Some decades later, the Canadian-based psychoanalyst Dr George Zavitzianos published a study of a 20-year-old psychopathic woman called 'Lillian' who sat in her father's car, naked, exhibiting herself to passers-by.[104] Unsurprisingly, 'Lillian' used to walk around naked as a little girl.[105]

Dr Estela Welldon, the eminent forensic psychotherapist and psychiatrist, completely challenged early psychoanalytical ideas about the seeming absence of exhibitionistic perversions and other forms of sexual perversions in the female.[106] In her landmark publication, *Mother, Madonna, Whore: The Idealization and Denigration of Motherhood*,[107] the first book-length psychoanalytical study of female sexual perversions, Dr Welldon described, among other cases, the tale of Miss E, a 34-year-old woman who began to expose her genitalia to female authority figures, in particular, from the age of 17 years. In order to flash, Miss E wore a special overcoat, and she derived great pleasure from shocking her victims, including her doctors, whom she tracked to their private homes. Over the years, Miss E's exhibitionism resulted in expulsion from schools, jobs, training centres, even counselling groups and mental hospitals. Sadly, Miss E could not control her urges at all and, on one occasion, one of Miss E's victims slapped her.

Dr Welldon noted that during her developmental years, Miss E's mother would masturbate her, as well as the other siblings, as a means of pacifying the children. Miss E's mother actually confirmed this type of 'child-rearing' practice in a subsequent communication. The mother confessed, 'it was easier than to use a dummy'.[108] Mother had to endure beatings from her drunken husband and the rhythmical masturbation of her children brought her some gratification.

In view of such an early experience, Miss E grew to use sexualisation as a predominant mechanism of defence in her interactions, transforming complicated negotiations with authority figures into sexual encounters involving exhibitionism. Welldon has also conceptualised Miss E's stripping as a form of manic enactment. Furthermore, Miss E had identified with the aggressor, her mother, by pestering others in an inappropriately sexual manner, just as her own incestuous mother had done. Shrewdly, Welldon has observed that by choosing powerful women as her victims, Miss E had secretly hoped that her doctors and other such women would actually contain her, and become better mother-figures than her own mother. As Welldon has suggested: 'Her hope for a shocked response in her victims had to do with a hopeful outcome in which women in authority – symbolic mothers – would not respond like her own mother, using and exploiting her as a part-object.'[109]

The work of Estela Welldon has confirmed once and for all that exhibitionism, though perhaps more widespread among male patients, can never be the exclusive domain of men, and that women will also display sexual perversions, including exhibitionistic perversions. Furthermore, Dr Welldon's clinical researches demonstrate the widespread incidence of abuse and molestation in the backgrounds of so many forensic, perverse individuals.

Psychotherapeutic Treatment

In terms of treatment and rehabilitation, the many generations of psychotherapists and psychoanalysts have made great strides in providing psychologically orientated opportunities for exhibitionistic patients to receive help. Eschewing shaming programmes, hypnosis, pharmacotherapy and incarceration as first lines of defence, the psychoanalytically orientated psychotherapists have deployed traditional 'talking therapy' with often good results. Sometimes we have attempted to do so with zeal, as had occurred when Freud's disciple Princess Marie Bonaparte, one of the founders of psychoanalysis in France, encountered a flasher who had exposed himself to her in the Bois de Boulogne. According to members of her family, the Princess remained unperturbed, and she handed her business card to the exhibitionist, offering him a free psychoanalytical consultation. As one might imagine, the chap bolted with all due haste.[110]

Although sustained psychoanalytical treatment can work effectively with the exhibitionist, one must work through the strong defence mechanisms of splitting and denial utilised by the patient as a means of warding off discomfort and anxiety.[111] The defences can often be deeply entrenched, as we can detect in the case reported by the American psychologist Dr David Shapiro, who wrote: 'a middle-aged man with a long history of exposing himself briefly to young girls admits, indeed emphasizes, that he is a "weak" person, a person lacking in self-control. He says (in his defense) that he does this only when drinking. However, he expresses no wish or intention to stop drinking.'[112] Other exhibitionists will deny the offence by claiming to be urinating, for example.[113]

Fortunately, if one can sustain the treatment relationship, then both clinician and client will have the opportunity to proceed through three general phases: (1) denial of the severity of the offence; (2) recognition of the psychopathology of the exhibitionistic act; and (3) working through of the symptomatology and broader character structure.[114] Although we do not have the space to discuss treatment issues in this context, psychoanalytical workers have reported some very impressive results in the rehabilitation of the exhibitionist.[115] Dr Elif Gürisik's moving and convincing account[116] of a flasher called 'Peter', a 34-year-old man who exposed and masturbated himself two or three times daily, provides a good indication of the possibilities of treatment. In spite of his compulsive masturbation, exhibitionism and depression – all very understandable in terms of his history, which included a promiscuous mother who had sex with many men in front of 'Peter' – the patient ultimately made a very good recovery in weekly psychoanalytically orientated group psychotherapy in a clinic setting. After five years, 'Peter' ceased his flashing behaviours, although he remained in treatment for seven years in total to consolidate his progress. His impulsiveness of character became transformed into thoughtfulness, and he became a more mature person, indulging in fewer sadomasochistic encounters with lovers and with family members. Eventually, he became a fervent skier, and a competitive ballroom dancer, winning several medals. As Gürisik recognised, skiing and ballroom dancing served as healthy and non-violent sublimations for the patient's need to expose himself.

Concluding Remarks

One need not search far before one will encounter evidence of exhibitionism in daily life. Virtually every museum and art gallery will contain nude paintings and sculptures, practically every community will have its naturists or nudist beaches with genitalia on display, and every health club will boast a profusion of saunas and steam rooms, replete with naked bodies. Our cultural icons often practise versions of exhibitionism, ranging from the provocatively dressed actress and model Elizabeth Hurley and her famous 'safety pin' dress, which left little to the imagination, to the legendary Hollywood actor Errol Flynn, who kept his friends entertained by exhibiting his full erection at parties.[117] *The Full Monty*, a filmic festival of male genital exhibitionism, became one of the most celebrated motion pictures in the history of the British cinema, and it subsequently became a huge hit musical on Broadway. And during the summer of 2000 and 2001, the British public enjoyed the extraordinarily popular television programme *Big Brother*, in which eleven strangers exhibited themselves on camera, 24 hours a day, from a special compound in East London, to a highly voyeuristic public, achieving unprecedented ratings and media coverage. Roughly ten million people sat glued to their television sets for the final episode of the first series of the British version of *Big Brother* in 2000, suggesting an enormous reciprocal relationship between those who exhibit and those who watch.

Exhibitionism forms a very substantial part of adolescent subculture as well, evidenced by the penchant for 'streaking', and 'mooning' (displaying one's buttocks through a car window, for example), which one encounters frequently as part of football hooliganism. Anyone walking through London's West End on a Friday night or Saturday night would have to be visually impaired not to notice the profusion of drunken men urinating against the sides of buildings.

Our relatives in the animal kingdom display themselves with great regularity, as we know from observational studies of baboons, chimpanzees, gorillas and orang-utans.[118] The male peacock exhibits himself most of all, with his resplendently phallic tail, designed to attract the female of the species. As a number of psychiatric authors have suggested, exhibitionism may even form a part of our 'hard-wiring'.[119]

And yet, as we have seen, this natural tendency to display can often become perverted, and reach offensive, criminal proportions. Fortunately, more psychoanalytical theoreticians and clinicians have begun to derive an increasingly better understanding of the causes and consequences of clinical exhibitionism and, hence, have begun to develop more sophisticated ways of treating the exhibitionist in a psychotherapeutic situation.

Because of the dangers associated with exhibitionism in its criminal and clinical form, many of us have become utterly phobic about the potential rewards of healthier, more sublimated versions of exhibitionism. Many people, including seasoned mental health professionals, will suffer from what I have come to regard as *psychological inhibitionism*, a fearful reaction to exhibitionism, wherein the person in question becomes very inhibited indeed, maintaining a very low profile, not disturbing the status quo and never achieving one's healthy goals and desires. The psychological inhibitionist suffers because he or she will lead only *half* a life, so frightened of what colleagues and friends and family members might think. As a result of these terrors, the inhibitionist will hide his or her light under a bushel, in perpetuity, living in a claustrophobic state.[120]

Dr Martin Dysart, the protagonist from Peter Shaffer's classic play *Equus*, might be regarded as a prototypical psychological inhibitionist. First performed in 1973, *Equus*, of course, concerns the plight of a highly troubled young boy, Alan Strang, who, in a fit of rage, blinds six horses. His 'normal' psychiatrist, Dr Dysart, would never engage in such a grotesque act of psychopathology; and yet, Dr Dysart suffers, tremendously so, precisely because he cannot unleash his passions at all, and he comes to envy the energy and vitality – however misdirected – of his disturbed young patient. As I suggested in a lecture some years ago, Dysart suffers from what I have come to call *psychic anaemia*, a cousin to psychological inhibitionism, a situation whereby one permits oneself to become drained of sufficient passion and life-blood, so much so that one becomes almost pathologically 'normal'. Certainly, any attempt at exhibitionist display, however healthy, or sublimated, or creative, will be frowned upon by the pathologically normal psychological inhibitionist. To be frank, this seems a very great shame indeed.

Psychological inhibitionism exists hand in hand with attacks on creativity. The noted Viennese émigré psychoanalyst Dr Heinz Kohut remarked upon the danger of not honouring one's creative exhibitionistic tendencies. Kohut theorised that 'too strict a rein on an artist's exhibitionism will tend to interfere with his productivity'.[121] Similarly, the Parisian psychoanalyst Dr Joyce McDougall has provided us with a beautiful case involving just such a difficulty with artistic expression.[122] McDougall worked with a female patient called 'Cristina', a sculptress, who suffered from terrific fear of exhibiting her sculptures in public. She believed, quite irrationally, that if she did so, her mother would die. McDougall helped 'Cristina' to remember that at the age of five years, her parents went away for one week, leaving her in the care of a maid. Anxious at the separation from her parents, 'Cristina' defecated and kept her faeces in a cardboard box, for which she received a severe scolding from the maid. McDougall speculated that the faecal stools became the patient's first sculptures and that, in her young mind, they became associated with great shame, which became transferred onto all other forms of display. Fortunately, after a successful psychoanalytical treatment, 'Cristina' managed to work through her anxieties about exhibiting her artistic products, and she eventually proceeded to sculpt some very large and highly acclaimed pieces.

Historically, we have castigated the psychological exhibitionist. Anyone who has achieved any notoriety or celebrity, in whatever walk of life, often becomes the object of tremendous derision from those who, perhaps, would prefer to be in the limelight themselves. It seems to me that we have become excessively narrow-minded in our thinking to imagine that the art of being seen, being observed, being noticed, being appreciated and so forth, should be confined to the celebrity or the exhibitionist. Surely, in an emotionally literate society, everybody needs to be taken seriously, and we ought to endeavour to provide room so that each and every one of us can have an arena.

Of course, we must be wary of the dangers of obnoxious interpersonal exhibitionism, and of its more sinister clinical variety, but at the same time, we must overcome our fears of exhibiting the very best of ourselves. If, as a community, we can vanquish our psychic inhibitions, and then manage to bear the primitive envy that we might feel for the skills and talents of others, just imagine what an infinitely richer world we might be able to create for ourselves, and for our children.

Acknowledgements

I wish to express my warm thanks to Mr Ivan Ward, the Series Editor, for having very kindly invited me to contribute this volume to his excellent book series, and for having had the courtesy to make many valuable editorial suggestions. I would also like to extend my appreciation to all the staff at Icon Books for their diligence in producing the final text, especially Mr Jeremy Cox, Mr Andrew Furlow, Mr Duncan Heath and Ms Jennifer Rigby, and to Ms Alison Foskett for her meticulous copy-editing. I also thank the wonderful librarians at the Tate Library of Regent's College, and at the Tavistock Clinic Library of the Tavistock Centre, for years of unflagging bibliographical support. I also want to express my thanks to the Librarian at the Anna Freud Centre in London.

I dedicate this book to Dr Estela Welldon, Senior Consultant Psychiatrist in Psychotherapy at the Portman Clinic in London, and Honorary President for Life of the International Association for Forensic Psychotherapy. As my esteemed and cherished teacher in forensic psychotherapy, I thank Dr Welldon for serving as a truly inspiring and generous role model in treating the offender patient with unique compassion.

Notes

1. Quoted in Rooth, F.G., 'Some Historical Notes on Indecent Exposure and Exhibitionism', *Medico-Legal Journal*, 1970, vol. 38, p. 139.

2. Ibid., p. 136.

3. Ibid., p. 139.

4. Ibid., p. 137.

5. Lasègue, E.C., *L'Union Médicale*, 1877, vol. 23, pp. 709–14.

6. Vandereycken, W. and van Deth, R., 'A Tribute to Lasègue's Description of Anorexia Nervosa (1873), with Completion of its English Translation', *British Journal of Psychiatry*, 1990, vol. 157, pp. 902–8.

7. See ibid. and Vandereycken, W. and van Deth, R., 'Who was the First to Describe Anorexia Nervosa: Gull or Lasègue?', *Psychological Medicine*, 1989, vol. 19, pp. 837–45.

8. Caprio, F.S. and Brenner, D.R., *Sexual Behavior: Psycho-Legal Aspects*, New York: Citadel Press, 1961.

9. See Langevin, R. and Lang, R.A., 'The Courtship Disorders', in Wilson, G.D. (ed.), *Variant Sexuality: Research and Theory*, Beckenham, Kent: Croom Helm, 1987, pp. 202–28.

10. American Psychiatric Association, *Diagnostic and Statistical Manual of Mental Disorders. Fourth Edition*, Washington, D.C.: American Psychiatric Association, 1994.

11. Rooth, F.G., 'Indecent Exposure and Exhibitionism', *British Journal of Hospital Medicine*, 1971, vol. 38, pp. 135–9.

12. See Rosen, I., 'Exhibitionism, Scopophilia and Voyeurism', in Rosen, I. (ed.), *The Pathology and Treatment of Sexual Deviation: A Methodological Approach*, London: Oxford University Press, 1964, pp. 293–350.

13. Abel, G.G. and Rouleau, J.L., 'The Nature and Extent of Sexual Assault', in Marshall, W.L., Laws, D.R. and Barbaree, H.E. (eds), *Handbook of Sexual Assault: Issues, Theories, and Treatment of the Offender*, New York: Plenum Press, 1990, pp. 9–21.

14. MacDonald, J.M., *Indecent Exposure*, Springfield, Illinois: Charles C. Thomas, 1973.

15. Jones, I.H. and Frei, D., 'Provoked Anxiety as a Treatment of Exhibitionism', *British Journal of Psychiatry*, 1977, vol. 131, pp. 295–300.

16. Snaith, P., 'Exhibitionism: A Clinical Conundrum', *British Journal of Psychiatry*, 1983, vol. 143, pp. 231–5.

17. Rhoads, J.M. and Borjes, E.P., 'The Incidence of Exhibitionism in Guatemala and the United States', *British Journal of Psychiatry*, 1981, vol. 139, pp. 242–4.

18. See Cox, D.J., 'Exhibitionism: An Overview', in Cox, D.J. and Daitzman, R.J. (eds), *Exhibitionism: Description, Assessment, and Treatment*, New York: Garland S.T.P.M. Press, 1980, pp. 3–10.

19. Cox, D.J. and McMahon, B., 'Incidents of Male Exhibitionism in the United States as Reported by Victimized Female College Students', *International Journal of Law and Psychiatry*, 1978, vol. 1, pp. 453–7.

20. Blair, C.D. and Lanyon, R.I., 'Exhibitionism: Etiology

and Treatment', *Psychological Bulletin*, 1981, vol. 89, pp. 439–63.

21. Lasègue (1877), op. cit.

22. Snaith, P. and Collins, S.A., 'Five Exhibitionists and a Method of Treatment', *British Journal of Psychiatry*, 1981, vol. 138, pp. 126–30.

23. Caprio and Brenner (1961), op. cit.

24. Myers, W.A., 'The Course of Treatment of a Case of Photoexhibitionism in a Homosexual Male', in Socarides, C.W. and Volkan, V.D. (eds), *The Homosexualities and the Therapeutic Process*, Madison, Connecticut: International Universities Press, 1991, pp. 241–9.

25. Ibid., quote, p. 241.

26. Christoffel, H., 'Male Genital Exhibitionism', in Lorand, S. and Balint, M. (eds), *Perversions: Psycho-dynamics and Therapy*, New York: Random House, 1956, pp. 243–64.

27. Cordess, C., 'Nuisance and Obscene Telephone Calls', in Bluglass, R. and Bowden, P. (eds), *Principles and Practice of Forensic Psychiatry*, Edinburgh: Churchill Livingstone, 1990, pp. 677–82.

28. Abel, G.G. and Osborn, C., 'The Paraphilias: The Extent and Nature of Sexually Deviant and Criminal Behavior', *Psychiatric Clinics of North America*, 1992, vol. 15, pp. 675–87.

29. Quoted in Allen, C., *A Textbook of Psychosexual Disorders*, London: Oxford University Press, 1962, p. 149.

30. Gittleson, N.L., Eacott, S.E. and Mehta, B.M.,

'Victims of Indecent Exposure', *British Journal of Psychiatry*, 1978, vol. 132, pp. 61–6.

31. Cox and McMahon (1978), op. cit.

32. Abel and Rouleau (1990), op. cit.

33. Arieff, A.J. and Rotman, D.B., 'Psychiatric Inventory of One Hundred Cases of Indecent Exposure', *Archives of Psychiatry and Neurology*, 1942, vol. 47, pp. 495–6.

34. Mohr, J.W., Turner, R.E. and Jerry, M.B., *Pedophilia and Exhibitionism: A Handbook,* Toronto: University of Toronto Press, 1964.

35. Gürisik, Ü.E., 'The Flasher', in Welldon, E.V. and Van Velsen, C. (eds), *A Practical Guide to Forensic Psychotherapy*, London: Jessica Kingsley Publishers, 1997, pp. 155–60.

36. Cox, D.J. and Maletzky, B.M., 'Victims of Exhibitionism', in Cox, D.J. and Daitzman, R.J. (eds) (1980), op. cit., pp. 289–93.

37. Abse, L., personal communication to the author, 24 October 2000.

38. Sugarman, P., Dumughn, C., Saad, K., Hinder, S. and Bluglass, R., 'Dangerousness in Exhibitionists', *Journal of Forensic Psychiatry*, 1994, vol. 5, pp. 287–96.

39. Masters, B., *The Shrine of Jeffrey Dahmer*, London: Hodder and Stoughton, 1993, p. 70.

40. Allen (1962), op. cit.

41. Flor-Henry, P. and Lang, R., 'Qualitative EEG Analysis in Genital Exhibitionists', *Annals of Sex Research*, 1988, vol. 1, pp. 48–62.

42. See Flor-Henry, P., 'Cerebral Aspects of Sexual Deviation', in Wilson, G.D. (ed.), *Variant Sexuality: Research and Theory*, Beckenham, Kent: Croom Helm, 1987, pp. 49–83.

43. Jones, I.H. and Frei, D., 'Exhibitionism: A Biological Hypothesis', *British Journal of Medical Psychology*, 1979, vol. 52, pp. 63–70.

44. Bluglass, R., 'Indecent Exposure in the West Midlands', in West, D.J. (ed.), *Sex Offenders in the Criminal Justice System*, Cambridge: Cambridge University Press, 1980, pp. 171–80.

45. Gelder, M., Gath, D. and Mayou, R., *Oxford Textbook of Psychiatry*, Oxford: Oxford University Press, 1983.

46. Quoted in Strozier, C.B., Interview with Eileen O'Shea, 10 December 1997, cited in Strozier, C.B., *Heinz Kohut: The Making of a Psychoanalyst*, New York: Farrar, Straus and Giroux, 2001, p. 324.

47. See Title 28, Section 28.567 of the 1954 Michigan Statutes Annotated, cited in Caprio and Brenner (1961), op. cit.

48. Allen (1962), op. cit.

49. Snaith and Collins (1981), op. cit.

50. Gayford, J.J., 'Indecent Exposure: A Review of the Literature', *Medicine, Science and the Law*, 1981, vol. 21, pp. 233–42. Cordess, C., 'Crime and Mental Disorder: I. Criminal Behaviour', in Chiswick, D. and Cope, R. (eds), *Seminars in Practical Forensic Psychiatry*, London: Gaskell, 1995, pp. 14–51.

51. Bianchi, M.D., 'Fluoxetine Treatment of Exhibitionism', *American Journal of Psychiatry*, 1990, vol. 147, pp. 1089–90. Maletzky, B.M., 'Exhibitionism: Assessment and Treatment', in Laws, D.R. and O'Donohue, W. (eds), *Sexual Deviance: Theory, Assessment, and Treatment*, New York: Guilford Press, 1997, pp. 40–74.

52. Gayford (1981), op. cit.

53. Evans, D.R., 'Electrical Aversion Therapy', in Cox, D.J. and Daitzman, R.J. (eds), *Exhibitionism: Description, Assessment, and Treatment*, New York: Garland S.T.P.M. Press, 1980, pp. 85–122.

54. Daitzman, R.J. and Cox, D.J., 'An Extended Case Report: The Nuts and Bolts of Treating an Exhibitionist', in Cox, D.J. and Daitzman, R.J. (eds), *Exhibitionism: Description, Assessment, and Treatment*, New York: Garland S.T.P.M. Press, 1980, pp. 253–85.

55. Jones and Frei (1977), op. cit.

56. Stevenson, J. and Jones, I.H., 'Behavior Therapy Technique for Exhibitionism: A Preliminary Report', *Archives of General Psychiatry*, 1972, vol. 27, pp. 839–41.

57. Jones and Frei (1977), op. cit., p. 298.

58. Wickramasekera, I., 'Aversive Behavior Rehearsal: A Cognitive-Behavioral Procedure', in Cox, D.J. and Daitzman, R.J. (eds), *Exhibitionism: Description, Assessment, and Treatment*, New York: Garland S.T.P.M. Press, 1980, pp. 123–49.

59. Ibid., p. 131.

60. Jones and Frei (1977), op. cit.

61. Quoted in Caprio and Brenner (1961), op. cit., p. 174.

62. Quoted in Caprio and Brenner (1961), op. cit., pp. 174–5.

63. Christoffel (1956), op. cit.

64. Freud, S., *The Interpretation of Dreams* (1900a), in Freud, S., *The Standard Edition of the Complete Psychological Works of Sigmund Freud. Volume IV (1900). The Interpretation of Dreams (First Part)*, Strachey, J., Freud, A., Strachey, A. and Tyson, A. (eds and trans.), London: Hogarth Press and The Institute of Psycho-Analysis, 1953, pp. xxiii–338. Freud, S., *The Interpretation of Dreams* (1900b), in Freud, S., *The Standard Edition of the Complete Psychological Works of Sigmund Freud. Volume V (1900–1901). The Interpretation of Dreams (Second Part) and On Dreams*, Strachey, J., Freud, A., Strachey, A. and Tyson, A. (eds and trans.), London: Hogarth Press and The Institute of Psycho-Analysis, 1953, pp. 339–625.

65. Freud (1900a), op. cit., p. 244.

66. Freud, S., *Three Essays on the Theory of Sexuality* (1905), in Freud, S., *The Standard Edition of the Complete Psychological Works of Sigmund Freud. Volume VII (1901–1905). A Case of Hysteria, Three Essays on Sexuality and Other Works*, Strachey, J., Freud, A., Strachey, A. and Tyson, A. (eds and trans.), London: Hogarth Press and The Institute of Psycho-Analysis, 1953, pp. 130–243.

67. Ibid., p. 165.

68. Freud, S., 'Draft H: Paranoia' (1895), pp. 206–12, in

Freud, S., Extracts from the Fliess Papers, in Freud, S., *The Standard Edition of the Complete Psychological Works of Sigmund Freud. Volume I (1886–1899). Pre-Psycho-Analytical Publications and Unpublished Drafts*, Strachey, J., Freud, A., Strachey, A. and Tyson, A. (eds and trans.), London: Hogarth Press and The Institute of Psycho-Analysis, 1966, pp. 177–280.

69. Freud, S., 'Medusa's Head' (1922), in Freud, S., *The Standard Edition of the Complete Psychological Works of Sigmund Freud: Volume XVIII (1920–1922). Beyond the Pleasure Principle, Group Psychology and Other Works*, Strachey, J., Freud, A., Strachey, A. and Tyson, A. (eds and trans.), London: Hogarth Press and The Institute of Psycho-Analysis, 1955, pp. 273–4.

70. Stekel, W., 'Zur Psychologie des Exhibitionismus', *Zentralblatt für Psychoanalyse*, 1911, vol. 1, pp. 494–5.

71. See Freud, S., Footnote, p. 495, in Stekel, W., 'Zur Psychologie des Exhibitionismus', *Zentralblatt für Psychoanalyse*, 1911, vol. 1, pp. 494–5.

72. Abraham, K., 'Restrictions and Transformations of Scopophilia in Psycho-Neurotics; with Remarks on Analogous Phenomena in Folk Psychology' (1913), in Abraham, K., *Selected Papers of Karl Abraham M.D.*, Bryan, D. and Strachey, A. (trans.), London: Hogarth Press and The Institute of Psycho-Analysis, 1927, p. 169.

73. Abraham, K., 'Ejaculatio Praecox' (1917), in Abraham (1927), op. cit., pp. 280–98.

74. Quoted in Freud (1900a), op. cit., p. 216.

75. Ferenczi, S., 'Spektrophobie', *Internationale Zeitschrift für Psychoanalyse*, 1915, vol. 3, p. 293.

76. Ferenczi, S., 'Die Nacktheit als Schreckmittel', *Internationale Zeitschrift für Psychoanalyse*, 1919, vol. 5, pp. 303–5.

77. Hárnik, J., 'The Various Developments Undergone by Narcissism in Men and Women', *International Journal of Psycho-Analysis*, 1924, vol. 5, pp. 66–83.

78. Lorand, S., 'The Psychology of Nudism', *Psychoanalytic Review*, 1933, vol. 20, pp. 197–207.

79. Rosen (1964), op. cit., p. 299.

80. Freud, A., 'Diagnosis and Assessment of Childhood Disturbances', *Journal of the Philadelphia Association of Psychoanalysis*, 1974, vol. 1, pp. 54–67.

81. Sterne, L., *The Life and Opinions of Tristram Shandy, Gentleman*, 9 vols, London, 1767.

82. Christoffel, H., 'Exhibitionism and Exhibitionists', *International Journal of Psycho-Analysis*, 1936, vol. 17, pp. 321–45. Christoffel (1956), op. cit.

83. Fenichel, O., *The Psychoanalytic Theory of Neurosis*, New York: W.W. Norton and Company, 1945.

84. Freud (1905), op. cit.

85. Winnicott, D.W., 'This Feminism' (1964), in Winnicott, D.W., *Home is Where We Start From: Essays by a Psychoanalyst*, Winnicott, C., Shepherd, R. and Davis, M. (eds), Harmondsworth, Middlesex: Penguin Books, 1986, p. 186. cf. Winnicott, D.W., 'The Concept of a Healthy Individual', in Sutherland, J.D. (ed.), *Towards Community*

Mental Health, London: Tavistock Publications, 1971, pp. 1–15.

86. Glasser, M., 'The Role of the Superego in Exhibitionism', *International Journal of Psychoanalytic Psychotherapy*, 1978, vol. 7, pp. 333–53.

87. Lucas, C., 'Exhibitionism', *British Journal of Psychotherapy*, 1990, vol. 7, pp. 15–24.

88. Ibid., p. 23.

89. See Socarides, C.W., 'The Demonified Mother: A Study of Voyeurism and Sexual Sadism', *International Review of Psycho-Analysis*, 1974, vol. 1, pp. 187–95.

90. See Socarides, C., 'D.W. Winnicott and the Understanding of Sexual Perversions', in Kahr, B. (ed.), *Forensic Psychotherapy and Psychopathology: Winnicottian Perspectives*, London: Karnac Books, 2001, pp. 95–109.

91. Lorand (1933), op. cit.

92. Caprio, F.S., 'A Case of Exhibitionism with Special Reference to the Family Setting', *American Journal of Psychotherapy*, 1948, vol. 2, pp. 587–602.

93. cf. Caprio and Brenner (1961), op. cit.

94. Caprio (1948), op. cit., p. 591.

95. Stoller, R.J., 'Centerfold: An Essay on Excitement', *Archives of General Psychiatry*, 1979, vol. 36, pp. 1019–24.

96. Lucas (1990), op. cit.

97. cf. Christoffel (1936), op. cit., Fenichel (1945), op. cit.

98. Stoller, R.J., *Perversion: The Erotic Form of Hatred*, New York: Pantheon Books, 1975. Stoller, R.J., *Observing*

the Erotic Imagination, New Haven, Connecticut: Yale University Press, 1985.

99. Allen (1962), op. cit.

100. Lucas (1990), op. cit.

101. Myers (1991), op. cit.

102. Rosen (1964), op. cit., p. 293.

103. Fenichel (1945), op. cit.

104. Zavitzianos, G., 'Fetishism and Exhibitionism in the Female and their Relationship to Psychopathy and Kleptomania', *International Journal of Psycho-Analysis*, 1971, vol. 52, pp. 297–305.

105. cf. Hollender, M.H., Brown, C.W. and Roback, H.B., 'Genital Exhibitionism in Women', *American Journal of Psychiatry*, 1977, vol. 134, pp. 436–8. Zavitzianos, G., 'More on Exhibitionism in Women', *American Journal of Psychiatry*, 1977, vol. 134, p. 820. Grob, C.S., 'Female Exhibitionism', *Journal of Nervous and Mental Disease*, 1985, vol. 173, pp. 253–6.

106. See Welldon, E.V., 'Contrasts in Male and Female Sexual Perversions', in Cordess, C. and Cox, M. (eds), *Forensic Psychotherapy: Crime, Psychodynamics and the Offender Patient. Volume II: Mainly Practice*, London: Jessica Kingsley Publishers, 1996, pp. 273–89.

107. Welldon, E.V., *Mother, Madonna, Whore: The Idealization and Denigration of Motherhood*, London: Free Association Books, 1988.

108. Ibid., quote, p. 96.

109. Ibid., p. 97.

110. Vickers, H., *Alice: Princess Andrew of Greece*, London: Hamish Hamilton, 2000.

111. Stoller (1985), op. cit. Pfäfflin, F., 'The Out-Patient Treatment of the Sex Offender', in Cordess, C. and Cox, M. (eds), *Forensic Psychotherapy: Crime, Psychodynamics and the Offender Patient. Volume II: Mainly Practice*, London: Jessica Kingsley Publishers, 1996, pp. 261–71.

112. Shapiro, D., *Dynamics of Character: Self-Regulation in Psychopathology*, New York: Basic Books, 2000, p. 61.

113. Murphy, W.D., 'Exhibitionism: Psychopathology and Theory', in Laws, D.R. and O'Donohue, W. (eds), *Sexual Deviance: Theory, Assessment, and Treatment*, New York: Guilford Press, 1997, pp. 22–39.

114. See Warren, M.P., *Behavioral Management Guide: Essential Treatment Strategies for Adult Psychotherapy*, Northvale, New Jersey: Jason Aronson, 2001.

115. e.g. Rosen (1964), op. cit. Socarides, C.W., *The Preoedipal Origin and Psychoanalytic Therapy of Sexual Perversions*, Madison, Connecticut: International Universities Press, 1988.

116. Gürisik (1997), op. cit.

117. Gansberg, A.L., Wallace, I., Wallace, A., Wallechinsky, D. and Wallace, S., 'In Like Flynn: Errol Flynn (June 20, 1909–Oct. 14, 1959)', in Wallace, I., Wallace, A., Wallechinsky, D. and Wallace, S. (eds), *The Intimate Sex Lives of Famous People*, New York: Delacorte Press, 1981, pp. 17–19.

118. Maletzky (1997), op. cit.

119. Jones and Frei (1979), op. cit.

120. Meltzer, D., *The Claustrum: An Investigation of Claustrophobic Phenomena*, Oxford: Clunie Press, 1992. Kahr, B., 'Winnicott's Recipe for the Good Life: Healthy Loving, Healthy Working, and Healthy Playing. The Madeleine Davis Memorial Lecture', The Squiggle Foundation, London, 15 May 1999.

121. Kohut, H., *The Analysis of the Self: A Systematic Approach to the Psychoanalytic Treatment of Narcissistic Personality Disorders*, New York: International Universities Press, 1971, p. 309.

122. McDougall, J., 'Creativity and Sexuality', in Richards, A.K. and Richards, A.D. (eds), *The Spectrum of Psychoanalysis: Essays in Honor of Martin S. Bergmann*, Madison, Connecticut: International Universities Press, 1994, pp. 373–90.